Table of Contents

4 Ways to Prepare Your Brand to Create Stunning Social Media Images (Even If You're in a "Boring" Industry)

Whilst images are hugely prevalent on social media, not all are created equal. Anybody can snap a quick photo, post it to social media and *maybe* it'll be received well, but most often the most effective examples of visuals are not ad-hoc or improvised creations. To achieve the greatest impact possible, it is important to plan ahead with the kind of visual content that will best resonate with your target audience. Here are a few strategies to help you do that, whether your business' visual content inspiration is obvious (fashion retailer, tourism board, organic fruit market...) or if it might need a bit more thought (financial services, portable toilets, wood burner log preparation...).

Re-visit your business idea, become your own customer

Think back to a time when your current business was just a twinkle in your eye, and you'll probably remember sitting down to brainstorm in detail why it is you were setting up in the first place. You'll have imagined your target customer, the things they needed, and how you planned to help them. Whether you still have these ideas written down or even if they only exist in your head, I encourage you to revisit them. Place yourself in the shoes of a customer and visualize their frame of mind. When you have completed this, scribble down some fresh thoughts about your customer base: the challenges they face, their wants and desires, their thoughts and feelings, and how you help overcome them. I know it all sounds a bit strange, but you will often find a renewed sense of focus and clarity that is easily lost in the hustle and bustle of everyday business. This strategy is useful in helping you to re-connect with the people who rely on you, and think in more human terms when it comes to visual content.

Ask and listen to your audience

Now that you have a clearer idea of what your customer wants, it's time to test that theory to make double sure. The easiest ways to do this are simply to ask and listen. Asking might involve asking simple or probing questions on social media, requesting feedback in your store, or sending out a request to your e-mail list. Ask a variety of questions to gather information, and then collate the responses so that you can analyze them to either confirm or re-align your business goals. While this strategy asks for active participation, you can also learn a lot simply by listening to what your audience is already saying about you. Going online is once again one of the best ways to facilitate this. Some examples include noting the emotional themes from customer service e-mails, searching Twitter for mentions of your brand name and the associated comments, seeing what people write on your Facebook Page, or underneath your YouTube videos.

Define your brand image (values, lifestyle)

There's no doubting that the makeup of your customer is central to the direction of your business (it wouldn't exist with them, after all), but you should not disregard your own values either, especially when it comes to visual marketing. In many cases, great influence can be had via the ideals that your brand evokes, the lifestyle that it encourages people to explore, or the history that led you to where you are today. In addition, your tone of voice, choice of colors, and overall themes should help to compound these principles. When you have a clearly defined set of beliefs and invite your audience to share in them too, they feel a greater affinity with your brand and products or services. This emotional investment makes them much more willing to engage with and share mentions of your brand on social media, because they want to project a certain image of themselves to their family and friends, and hopefully they are proud to as well.

Assess your goals and measure return on investment

As with any new marketing initiative - especially one as radical as optimizing your visual output on social media - it is important to begin with an idea of what you hope to achieve and how that fits into your overall marketing goals, whether that be brand awareness, increased loyalty, positive press, lead generation, improved levels of engagement, etc. If you are already measuring your return on investment (ROI), mark a baseline and see how things have changed a few weeks and months down the line. If you are not yet analyzing your activity, definitely make a decision to start, otherwise you'll never know exactly how well (or badly!) you are doing, and won't be able to accurately tweak your strategy as time goes on. There are a myriad of tools to help you track social media ROI, but for most people, simple tools like Facebook and YouTube's built-in analytics, Google Analytics, and sites like the link-shortening tool bit.ly - which comes with free stats - will more than suffice.

The 10 Key Principles of Successful Social Media Images

When they are picked apart, the most successful examples of visuals on social media are underpinned by a number of key principles. Ten of these principles are detailed below, and while they might not all apply to every single piece of visual content, generally most of them do. When you read the following, start thinking about how you can align this with your own social media strategy.

1. Create beautiful visuals

This one is a given. If you're going to stand out amongst the crowd on social media, the visuals that you create must be of a high standard. Hiring photographers, graphic designers, and videographers is one (very expensive) option to get the job done, but you can just as easily create stunning content for next-to-nothing (or free!) with some basic knowledge of photography theory, coupled with the myriad of creation and enhancement tools that are available online and on your mobile phone. High quality, relevant images make your marketing easier to understand and reflect your company's professionalism, so say good bye to the days of cheesy stock images (unless used ironically, of course!). When you're genuinely passionate about your brand and the visual content you create, that care and enthusiasm will filter through to your audience - and even if it takes a while for you to hit your full stride, that's something money cannot buy.

The vacuum manufacturer, Dyson, takes great care in the way it structures its images on social media, producing scenes that its customers can imagine as being part of their everyday lives. In the following example to used to demonstrate how effective its technology is at tackling pet hair, a homely setting with complementary colors and clear branding (including hashtag) is used to show how Dyson products can help to make people's lives easier: http://bit.ly/dysonpet

2. Be valuable and helpful

This principle links to the first, and also harks back to the last chapter where we discussed how weaving your brand values into visual storytelling makes for better content. Every business strives to be the best they can be, but *also* be better than the competition. On social media, building trust, credibility (and driving purchases) through valuable, personable, and helpful posts is a major part of becoming numero uno in your field; it's a strategy that applies to all aspects of content creation on social platforms, and strong and memorable visuals can really help hammer the point home.

In the following examples, the dishwasher tablet brand, Cascade, pairs images of sparkling clean crockery with tips on how to get the best results with its product:

Cascade building trust and credibility

http://bit.ly/cascadetip1
http://bit.ly/cascadetip2

3. Keep messages simple

In order to keep your visual marketing as impactful as possible, try not to overcomplicate the message each piece of content is trying to tell. Ideally, your images should communicate a single idea that can be easily digested; anything more and you are at risk of confusing people, diluting its meaning, and reducing "shareability." Research by Buffer found that self-explanatory, stand-alone social media images perform better than those that need explanation and clarification in the accompanying description.[4] When the travel company Expedia promotes holiday destinations on Pinterest, it lets simple and beautiful images speak for themselves:

Expedia keeping the visuals simple to inspire customers:
http://bit.ly/expedia1
http://bit.ly/expedia2a
http://bit.ly/expedia3

4. Focus on "shareability"

Central to the wider success of a lot of visual content is how much it is shared on social media to friends, family, and other connections. People share stuff they see online for a number of reasons, whether it is selfless (e.g. to pass on something entertaining or eye-opening) or somewhat selfish (to characterize themselves and their personality to be viewed by others in a certain way). For each piece of content you create, ask yourself what value it will provide, and consider if it is something that your audience will want to share.

In a successful take on the "Nailed it" meme, in which an image of an impressive feat is juxtaposed with a humorously bad attempt at re-creating it, Mountain Dew paired a glorious example of a ship in a bottle with its own shoddy attempt (complete with the scissors used to cut open the bottle and the tape used to seal it back up): http://bit.ly/mountaindewship This image - and memes in general - are incredibly shareable because, as well as being funny, they trigger a "I know that feeling" response in a lot of us that we think our friends will recognize, too.

5. Be emotive and human

What so often makes visual marketing so much more powerful than text is how it can instantaneously appeal to people's emotions, whether overtly or subconsciously. For the majority of the time, you'll want to elicit a positive reaction through content that is funny, inspiring, cute, etc. However, bringing out negative feelings in your audience such as anger, shock, or fear can be just as impactful if they can be channelled in an optimistic or constructive way - charity appeal adverts are very effective at this. In addition, it is imperative that you let your brand's human side come out in your tone of voice and the content you choose to produce - make an effort to match both to the audience and sites you are posting to, heavily restrict direct selling and actively become a part of your own tribe.

In a simple, yet powerful example of this strategy, The Home Depot posted a collage of photos of US military personnel receiving its Herobox care packages whilst out on deployment. The response from customers was overwhelmingly positive, with thousands of people commenting on how proud they were of their men and women in uniform and complimenting The Home Depot on its generous act: http://bit.ly/thehomedepot1

6. Create a sense of urgency... or don't

This is probably the one principle listed here that I don't think will necessarily apply to all types of visual content. Fabricating a sense of urgency has long been used in advertising as a way to encourage people to take action ("Sale ends in 24 hours - buy now!"), and depending on the message you are trying to impart in any single piece of visual storytelling, it *could* be effective. Just as powerful, however, are stories that encourage people to take a few moments to think, pause and reflect. This is especially relevant in a world where our lives are so non-stop, people's morale might be low or mind consumed by stress, and your message gives them the alternative perspective or pick-me-up that they so badly needed.

The fast food chain Chick Fil-A posted a photo of its 93-year-old founder speaking to a young child in one of its restaurants along with the caption *"Love what you do, and you'll never work a day in your life."* The candidness of the image along with a phrase that really makes people stop and think about their own lives, was a very effective combination: http://bit.ly/chickfila1

7. Make content platform-specific

Producing great social media marketing content takes time; a precious commodity for all businesses. While I am a strong advocate of creating one image, graphic, presentation etc. and re-purposing it across several channels, I also strongly advise that the said content is tweaked to align itself to make the most of each platform's strengths and best appeal to the sites' different audiences.

Nike executes this concept well with its Nike Training Club brand, showcasing the same product in slightly different ways across several social networks and using a visual style that best suits the structure and audience of each. Take a look at the following example:

Nike Magical Kaleidoscope Tights

Facebook: http://bit.ly/niketraining1

Pinterest: http://bit.ly/niketraining2
Instagram: http://bit.ly/niketraining3

8. Tell a story

In a book about visual marketing with an emphasis on storytelling, you might be rolling your eyes at the heading above. However, it pays to remember that when you create image-centric content, it is important to compliment the visual element with a strong narrative that reflects the personality and vision of your brand and its customers. After all, as explained eariler, whether through the spoken word or images, humans communicate and understand the world through stories.

Vans posted the following photo on Instagram of someone wearing a battered up pair of its shoes. Everybody can relate to an item of well-worn footwear that they are reluctant to throw away. They're with us everywhere we go and their rips, scuffs, and marks remind of us of a myriad of memories: http://bit.ly/vansoldshoes

9. Live in the moment and plan for the future

Some of the best visual marketing on social media occurs in the spur of the moment, based on unexpected moments in your day or topical news events that ignite a creative spark in your brain. Oreo is one brand that excels at this strategy, typified by its *"Power out? No problem. You can still dunk in the dark"* image posted to Twitter very soon after the electrical outage that hit the Super Bowl in 2013: http://bit.ly/oreopowercut

Where the future is concerned, think ahead with a content calendar and ideas about how you might use visual storytelling - linked to your brand - to mark significant cultural events, e.g. St' Patrick's Day, Valentine's Day, the Oscars, or holidays like Christmas and Easter.

10. Aim to go viral - whatever that means to you

If your visual post goes viral, you've hit the marketing jackpot... unless it spreads like wildfire for all of the wrong reasons, which I hope will never happen! It's almost impossible to judge in advance whether any particular post will explode in popularity, but by utilizing the advice above and learning from the examples to follow throughout this book, you'll be giving all of your content the best chance possible. Of course, it helps to celebrate every small win and to understand virality is often relative to the size of your potential audience.

5 Ways to Brand Your Images on Social Media

As a business, there are two main reasons why you should brand all of your social media images. Firstly, by marking an image as *made by you*, people will always be able to identify the original source of the content, even if - after being shared countless times across multiple social networks and websites - no one (as often happens) is bothering to give you either written or linked credit.

The second reason for branding your images stems from a much more immediate need: so that your brand's visual content can be instantly identifiable when it is posted to social networks. By consistently branding your images, you subtly teach your audience to recognise your content (which they know from previous experience is going to be worth their time), and to stop and engage with it in amongst all of the items in their crowded news feeds.

Let's take a look at 5 different ways that you can brand your social media images. Of course, some of these tactics will work better (and be more tolerated by the audience) on some social networks than for others.

1. Brand name or logo

This is one of the most obvious - just slap a big ol' logo on top of the image that you are sharing! If you *are* going to take this approach, I would suggest being cautious about the size and placement of your brand name or logo so that it does not detract from the power of the visual itself. Ideally, keep it small and place it in one of the corners. For additional subtlety and something more like a watermark than a solid stamp, consider using an image editing program to remove the colour from your logo and to make it slightly transparent. Alternatively, mark the image with a simple piece of text with your website or Facebook URL, or your Twitter handle. One brand that unashamedly plasters its logo onto social media images is *Pepsi*, particularly on Facebook (http://bit.ly/pepsibranding). In a strange sense, *Pepsi* is such a huge brand that it can get away with this kind of brash self-promotion, but as the pointers above suggest, it is not an approach that most brands - who are mostly aiming for their content to flow seamlessly into the social network streams of users - should necessarily go for.

2. Fonts

The type of font that you use in social media images can reveal to people a lot about the personality and culture of your brand, and used consistently, it can really help make your content stand out within people's news feeds. When deciding on a font, think carefully about how it will reflect on your brand and the message you want to project. Are you serious, fun, sarcastic, etc.? Before settling on a font (especially if you will be paying money for it), study the readability of its letters at different sizes, and pay attention to whether the font set includes bold and italic variations and special characters, which may come in handy later on down the line. The cosmetics brand, Lush, characterizes itself by one of two fonts, used consistently across all of its marketing. One is a simple, bold typeface, and the other is the following italicized typeface (http://bit.ly/lushbranding)

Note: The font I am talking about in this point is *not* the font you might have chosen for your brand's logo. I am specifically referring to a *different* typeface used to annotate images, make announcements, share motivational quotes, etc. Some of the best resources for free fonts include Dafont (http://www.dafont.com/) and Font Squirrel (http://www.fontsquirrel.com/).

3. Color palette

Some brands are synonymous with their own colours - the yellow and red of *McDonald's* (http://bit.ly/mcdonaldsbranding), the red and white of *Coca-Cola*, the blue and white of *Gap*, to name but three. All of these brands exploit this recognisability in their social media content, often posting images with bold or subtle mentions of these hues, because they know just how strongly their audience identifies with them. Whether it's a combination of two colours or more that are a mirror of your brand logo *or* reflection of your company's personality, this strategy is one other powerful way of helping your images to stand out and be recognised on social media. Here is a brief overview of some of the most commonly used color themes in images:

Neutral

Suited to natural and earthy content, dominated by browns and creams, emphasised by increased image transparency or decreased saturation. Check out how Aldo Shoes uses a plain white background in tandem with neutral-colored products to achieve an engaging image: http://bit.ly/aldoneutral

Pastel

Best suited to soft, elegant, or feminine content. Difficult to obtain a strong contrast between different pastel hues, so text will benefit from a semi-transparent background shape, like a white circle. In the following example, Tropicana uses complimenting pastel shades to create a bright, fresh, and appealing image: http://bit.ly/tropicanapastel

Monochrome

Effect uses several shades of the same colour. Often benefits from textured background to minimize "flatness" of overall image. Check out how Target uses multiple shades of green to add texture and interest to its "Happy Earth Day" image: http://bit.ly/targetmono Although the text is white, a very light shade of green would work, too.

Neon

Bright hues paired with bold text stand out on social media. Depending on the font color, neon can work against both light and dark backgrounds. Check out this example from Maybelline New York, used to promote mascara: http://bit.ly/socialmedianeon

Note: If you need some inspiration for the types of colors you might want to use - and pick a selection that complement each other nicely, check out the myriad of suggestions at Adobe's Kuler website https://kuler.adobe.com/. Use the color wheel here to concoct your own unique blend of flattering hues from scratch, or click on the "Explore" link to discover a myriad of suggestions for you to pick, edit, and play around with. Be sure to make a note of the RGB and Hex color codes so that you and your team members have the exact colors ready, whenever you need them. In addition, I am a big fan of the free tool ColorPic, which allows you to identify and "grab" any colour on-screen for use in your image creation, simply by hovering your mouse cursor over it. Download it here: http://www.iconico.com/colorpic/ ColorPic is only available for Windows, but Skala Color will do the same job if you're a Mac user. Download it here: http://bjango.com/mac/skalacolor/

4. Image border

One of the simplest ways to brand your images on social media is with a thin colored border around them. The Facebook Page 8Fact (http://www.facebook.com/8fact) frames all of its images with a solid, bright yellow line, helping to ensure that its daily content is recognizable to its audience when it goes live. If you feel like a full border might be a bit too much, you could take after the British supermarket, Sainsbury's. In a more subtle approach to 8Fact, it "underlines" the images it posts with a subtle orange graduated gradient (http://bit.ly/sainsburysbranding). This ensures that fans can identify the content as "owned" by the company, but it also gives the images considerably more breathing space; sometimes a full border can choke the image a little.

5. Filters

The rise of Instagram has given huge rise to the use of one-tap custom filters to change the mood and personality of an image. Where branding is concerned, consistent use of a particular filter can help to strengthen your brand's identity on social media. One important thing to remember with the use of filters is *not to go overboard*. As much as filters have the power to enhance an image, so too do they have the power to destroy it. Keep your use of filters subtle and restrained, so not too detract from the honesty of your visuals. For example, it is generally acceptable to use a filter to improve the look of a photo of a restaurant dish or a natural landscape, but if the colors of the food are unnatural or the scenery looks like it has been lifted from a computer-animated *Disney* movie, viewers are more likely to be suspicious or distrustful. One brand that uses image filters to good effect is the swimwear manufacturer, Tiger Lily (http://bit.ly/tigerlilybranding). Its consistent and subtle use of one type of filter helps to reflect its cool, relaxed, and "sunny" brand culture, and has the added effect of making its visuals more recognizable in people's news feeds.

The case for *not* branding images on social media

While the benefits of subtly branding your social media images are clear, there is a school of thinking that argues a case for dropping any form of image branding - on select occasions, at least. The idea is that when an image has no branding, people are more likely to share because they feel a greater sense of ownership over it - the visual content is suddenly much more selfless, or more about the fan and their connections than it is your brand.. In practice, this approach works best when paired with content that branding just wouldn't really fit with, either because they are historically or emotionally significant. High quality, original mages published to mark Martin Luther King Day or Mother's Day, for example, may be received more warmly without your logo or website plastered on them. While there is a greater risk that your unattributed image may be stolen to be used away from the social networks to which it is posted, as long as it *is* shared on these social networks, your brand name should appear alongside it.

Photos on Social Media: How to Snap Super Shots Every Time

With the prevalence of digital cameras and smartphones in modern life, everybody is a photographer. Some people are definitely better photographers than others, but the ability to instantly capture a moment and share it on social media has transformed the way that people express what is important to them in their lives, and brands can do the same.

As much as it pains me to admit it, I often see *terrible* photographs taken by businesses on social media - blurry, badly lit, poorly composed... the list goes on. When you're trying to show the best side of your company to the world, good quality photographs count. As we'll discuss a bit later on, your snaps don't have to be professionally staged to get attention, but you *should* take care to ensure that the photos you publish don't look like they were taken with no consideration for how they will connect with your customers. The following tips cover some very basic photography theory, but taking these guidelines (*not* fixed rules) into account can make a huge difference to how your images will be perceived:

Rule of thirds

Imagine that your image is divided into nine equal segments by two vertical and horizontal lines. The rule of thirds states that the most important elements of your scene should be positioned along these lines, or at the points that they intersect, in order to add balance and interest to your photos. In the following example from Tourism Australia, the sand, sea, and sky split the photo into three eye-pleasing segments (http://bit.ly/ruleofthirdsaustralia)

Leading lines

Whenever we look at photos, our eyes are naturally drawn to lines within them, whether that's the zig-zag of a mountain road or the positioning of a knife and fork next to a plate. Lines can be used strategically to pull our eyes into the picture, often towards the main subject. In this example from Gap, the straight lines created by the street and sidewalk direct our attention to the man modelling its clothes (http://bit.ly/gaplines)

Symmetry and pattern

The world is full of symmetry and pattern, and whether it occurs naturally (e.g. in the reflection of a mountain on the lake below it) or is manmade (e.g. in architecture, like windows on an old church), this kind of equilibrium is attractive to the human eye. In the following example from Whole Foods Market, symmetry is achieved by shooting a photograph at the corner of one of its buildings, and is also used as a way to reflect the image's caption which celebrates the opening of two new stores (http://bit.ly/wholefoodssymmetry)

Viewpoint

Where you stand when you take a photo can make a huge different to how people perceive it. Rather than *always* snapping from eye-level, get up high, down below, at the side or from the back, close to the subject or far away, to see how this changes the interest of, and message that your shot will convey. In the following example from Ford, positioning the camera behind the car with the mountains in the distance helps to foster a real sense of adventure - in particular, the adventure that said car will take drivers on (http://bit.ly/fordviewpoint).

Framing

If you've ever placed a border or frame around a painting or photograph, you'll know how much it can affect how the shot is perceived, helping to focus viewers' attention on the subject. The real world is full of objects that naturally create frames, like trees, buildings, and archways. In the following example from lululemon, powerful framing is created by - of all things - two signs warning of danger of death (http://bit.ly/luluframing).

Background

The background of your photographs can make a huge difference to the quality of the overall shot, either compounding the impact of the subject or inadvertently drawing all attention away from them. Consider whether the subject you want to shoot would benefit best from a busy or plain background, and adjust your composition accordingly. In the following example from Gucci, the plain yellow background works to make the subject (a handbag in a contrasting color) "pop" (http://bit.ly/guccibackground).

Cropping

Cropping a photo is often necessary in order to isolate the subject in order to prevent them from being lost in the noise of the surroundings. Try to strike a balance between cropping enough so to increase the appeal of the photo, whilst still using the background to enhance its visual appeal. The LEGO brand uses closely-cropped photographs as a necessity, in order to showcase the detail of its tiny figurines. In the following example, we get a good look at LEGO Santa Claus, and the impression that he is positioned in a messy workshop (http://bit.ly/legocropping).

Experiment and filter

Never accept the first photo you take. With digital cameras allowing you to take hundreds of photos without worrying about running out of film, don't be afraid to experiment with the composition of your photos multiple times before you find a shot that you are happy with. Maintain a decent standard of quality, and never post photos that will reflect badly on your brand, i.e. if you post blurry, badly lit images with no real focus - and this is how you present yourself publicly - how will this make people think you work behind the scenes? Despite posting lots of great photos, this example from Rustico Pizzeria - a non-square, over-exposed, frankly boring photo of a pizza slice - is not tempting me to indulge in its $1 slice night! http://bit.ly/badpizzapic

7 Types of Photographs that Your Social Media Fans Will Love

While many brands are used to releasing highly staged photos as part of carefully-planned (and often expensive) marketing campaign, social media gives you the chance to let loose and be more spontaneous. Customers are much more clued up about the way that professional photos can be manipulated before their public release, so while the odd "traditional" promotional shot won't do any harm, they will also very much appreciate images that show a more personal and "real" side to your business. In this chapter, we'll take a look at some of the best kinds of images to post on social media - many of which reflect the core lessons of being transparent, personable, and valuable that we covered earlier on in the book.

Advertise products and services

Nearly all brands are on social media to help sell their wares in one way or another, and photos of your product or service are an inevitable part of that. However, when you *do* share these types of shots, it usually (depending on the product and social networks) helps if you *don't* do it as you would for a catalogue or flyer, i.e. simply placing the item on a plain white background and publishing it to your fans with a "Buy now!" caption. Product shots taken in a more natural setting - like showing a rain coat being worn in a real shower of rain, a hose pipe being used in the back yard, or a real team of financial advisers hard at work in the office - tend to be received much better because they show how your wares fit into customers' everyday lives, aren't jarring and annoying in people's feeds, and can help to foster an emotional connection with your brand. In the following example, Starbucks uses a relaxed setting, coupled with a play on words in the image caption, to promote its macchiato coffee in an eye-catching and emotionally-appealing way (http://bit.ly/starbucksproduct).

Ask questions

Asking questions - anchored by an image (or four) - is a really simple and effective way of gathering information about the interests and needs of your audience, and using that to develop your products, services, and social media marketing strategy for the future. In addition, the easier you make it for people to respond to questions, the more likely they are to engage.

In the following example, artist Jody Gaul asks her Twitter fans to pick the greeting card design they like best from a choice of four. The image is split into four separate quadrants labelled A, B, C, D, and the accompanying text reads simply, "Which is your favorite? A, B, C or D?" http://bit.ly/jodyart

Show behind the scenes

There was a time, not too long ago, where the allure and magic of a product or service was in the fact that we *didn't* know how it worked. With the openness of social media, that has all changed, and audiences are now intrigued to go behind the curtain at your business and enjoy the feeling of privilege that they get from being invited into a place that most people do not normally get to see. They want to (and often demand to) know how your business works, and you should be in a position to let them in as a way to demonstrate your company's human side.

For example, the UK department store chain Harvey Nichols posted a photo on Twitter with the caption *"Behind the scenes insight into the preparation involved in serving our exquisite dishes #FoodiePhotos #RestaurantWeek"*, and a candid, impromptu photograph of one of its chefs hard at work (http://bit.ly/harleybts). Other types of behind-the-scenes shots might highlight some unsung members of staff or show a product in the planning stages, and they work much more effectively than any simple text could explain.

Offer hints and tips - photo collages work well

Offering hints and tips to your audience is a really effective way to remain consistently valuable, increase the potential virality of your posts, and to grow brand loyalty. One of the easiest ways to do this is to demonstrate simple step-by-step instructions by splitting a single image up into multiple frames.

Brands like The Home Depot are big advocates of this strategy, as it allows them to feature their products *and* be helpful at the same time. In the following example, The Home Depot uploaded a single image to Facebook, split into three. In pictures alone, it shows how customers can create a delightful centerpiece for summer parties. The image caption includes a link to the company's blog, where the DIY project is explained in more detail: http://bit.ly/hintsandtips1

Highlight your charitable side

As a way to enhance your brand image, use images to highlight your company's charitable side and its dedication to make a difference in the community it is a part of. In the following example, Wake Forest Sports Medicine in North Carolina posted a group photo of its staff as they took part in its annual Staff Service Day. Many customers appreciate it when a company shows that it has a caring side, and photos like this one - complete with lots of smiling faces and matching t-shirts - demonstrates that in spades: http://bit.ly/givebackws Of course, this strategy does not have to be carried out on a grand scale to be effective. Any example where you can demonstrate that you went beyond the call of duty to make someone's day a little bit better - and show it off in picture form - has the potential to do very well. One image that went viral showed a letter from one of Nike's big bosses; a reply to a customer who asked him to explain how the brand name should be pronounced. [5] This wasn't even shared by Nike on its social media channels, but you can bet when the customer got that reply, he certainly did, thus providing the sports brand with a whole load of free marketing.

User-generated images

What better way to share the visual story of your brand than involving your customers in a collaborative effort? Encouraging fans to share photos to show how your company is part of their lives is very influential marketing for new customers, and by highlighting such content on your social media profiles - which will also get liked and commented upon - you make said fans feel very special, indeed. The Kitchn - a daily web magazine devoted to home cooking and kitchen design- used this strategy around Thanksgiving, a time when it knew a lot of its fans would like to share images of their culinary creations. Their message to readers said:

"This Thanksgiving when you share your mashed potatoes and pumpkin pie with your friends and family, be sure to share some with us! We'd love to see what you're making this year. Simply use #thekitchn when you share your Thanksgiving photos on Instagram, or ask a question on Twitter. We'll reshare some of our favorite photos you send us, and retweet or respond to any last minute questions you might have."[6]

Asking fans to include a unique hashtag with their photos makes them much easier to find and re-purpose on their own account. The Kitchn uses a similar strategy on its Instagram account, regularly re-posting and crediting the photos of its fans.

Jump on photo-taking fads in popular culture

Just as the popularity of a meme comes and goes, so do real-life photo trends. Photobombing and selfies are trends that look like they are here to stay, but others like "whaling" and "owling" were transient, burning out as quickly as they arrived. Nevertheless, all of these trends can be taken advantage of in order to boost engagement, whether you take the photos yourself or encourage your fans to, so that you can share their efforts on your social profiles. For example, Currumbin Wildlife Sanctuary in Australia encourages visitors to take selfies with some of the animals within the park, which it then features on its Facebook and Instagram profiles (http://bit.ly/zooselfie).

10 Places to Find Totally Free, High Quality Photos to Use on Social Media

While snapping your own photos to use on social media is always the ideal scenario, oftentimes it just isn't possible due to time constraints, cost, and other factors. That's where using *other* people's images comes in. While there are a ton of excellent paid stock photo sites online, sometimes the expense (however little) can really start to add up. So, here are 10 totally free online resources for finding photos to use on social media. This is by no means a comprehensive list of the free image sources out there, but these are some of my favorites:

Searchable databases

1. Free Images

Free Images (http://www.freeimages.com/) describes itself as the leading source of free stock photos, and with over 400,000 to choose from, it probably has a strong case. Photos are keyword-searchable and categorized, but the sign-up and download process is a bit longer than some of the other options I have listed below. For the sheer amount of choice, though, it's probably worth the effort.

2. Free Digital Photos

Free Digital Photos (http://www.freedigitalphotos.net/) features a large selection of free images, categorized for your convenience. Small versions of the photographs come at no charge, but there is a fee for large copies, should you require them.

3. Public Domain Pictures

Public Domain Pictures (http://www.publicdomainpictures.net/) is a repository for a wide variety of free public domain images uploaded by amateur photographers. Sign-up is required, and a premium download option is available if you need larger images.

Free-form photo collections

Unlike the examples above, the following websites are smaller in scale, with a much more sporadic delivery of free images. Nevertheless, they're worth checking on in case you hit upon a great image when you least expect it, or for grabbing some photos to save for another day.

4. BigFoto

Most of BigFoto's (http://www.bigfoto.com/ royalty-free photos have been uploaded by amateur photographers for little or no personal gain. Images here are largely sorted by geographic area, although the "Themes" option (which includes categories like Nature, Food, Christmas, etc.) is a helpful addition.

5. Gratisography

Gratisography (http://www.gratisography.com/) offers free high-resolution photos that can be used for personal and commercial projects. No sign-up is required; simply click on an image to download, and more are added every week.

6. PicJumbo

PicJumbo (http://picjumbo.com/) is a project started by Viktor Hanacek, a web designer who realized his peers' need for high quality, full resolution photos, and wanted to do something to help. The website offers his own photos, completely free, and for any use. You don't *have* to credit the photos to him, but he does appreciate it if you do. There's no search engine on PicJumbo, but the categories listed in the menu bar will guide you sufficiently enough.

Image search websites

The following websites do not host free photos themselves, but rather provide a way to search the image hosting site Flickr, or public domain photos, to discover thousands free images for you to use. Well worth a gander:

7. CompFight

There are several websites that grab image results from Flickr, but CompFight (http://compfight.com/) is my favorite. Upon searching, use the options on the left to filter your photos by license type. When you've found the one you like, hover your cursor over it to check that its size will meet your needs), click the pic and use to check the license agreement and download the image in various sizes. If you're hosting the image on your website, you'll even find an automatically-generated snippet of HTML code to be copied and pasted, and that will generate the attribution for you.

8. CanWeImage

CanWeImage (https://canweimage.com/) is a personal project by one Tayler Summs, which allows you to search the Wikimedia Commons website for images. Wikimedia Commons is a massive database housing millions of free media files. The images on its native site are highly organized, but the site isn't the most user-friendly to navigate, which is why Summs' tool is so useful.

9. EveryStockPhoto

Providing a search engine to find millions of free photos across a number of different sources, EveryStockPhoto (http://www.everystockphoto.com/) is one of the longest-established websites of its kind. Along with clear licensing details for each photo, there's also a free, time-saving Firefox plugin available, so that you can search the site direct from your browser.

10. StockPhotos.io

StockPhotos.io (http://stockphotos.io) is a Creative Commons-licensed professional free stock photos sharing community, which currently houses around 25,000 high resolution images. All photos displayed on this Pinterest-esque site are allowed to be used for commercial use, as long as proper credit is given.

Graphics on Social Media: Ideas Your Audience Will Love

Combining any image with a text overlay is a quick, easy, and powerful way to communicate your message or to ensure that the caption associated with a visual is not overlooked, and that's how the term "graphic" is reflected throughout this chapter, whether the image is a photo, hand-drawn illustration, vector, or anything else. Let's look at some of the most popular and effective ways to use graphics on social media:

Motivational or inspirational quotes

The busier and more complicated our lives get, the more we seem to appreciate little words of wisdom to give us an emotional boost, or bring a sense of perspective to our lives. This type of content is so popular because it reaches people on an emotional level, and it is also highly shareable (when someone receives a snippet of inspiration or motivation, they will want to pass that on to benefit their friends, but *also* to give the impression that they are wise and a source of inspiration themselves). Of course, it also reflects well on your brand as you'll be seen as a go-to source for life-affirming snippets of information that resonate with your company values, and those of your customers. Motivational and inspirational quotes are available in abundance with a simple Google search - or you may have some of your own, spoken by employees of your company, either historically or recently at a conference or trade show. This type of content can either be displayed as text-only images, or the text can overlay a photo that is representative of the quote that is featured - whether that's an original image from you or one you find online. Everyday Health has a whole board dedicated to inspirational quotes on Pinterest, such as the following example, which is branded by font, color, and logo to make it identifiable as content "owned" by it: (http://bit.ly/everydayhealthinspiration)

Nostalgia and memories

One of the biggest points of connection between people (or brand and customer) is shared experiences and a sense of familiarity, particularly those from the past, and companies on social media can easily tap into these deep-rooted and powerful memories with graphics that revisit nostalgic moments.

These moments often relate to hobbies, home, work, and family life, from pop culture, or highlight the history and heritage of your business. Successful nostalgic photos trigger a specific feeling in the minds of their customers, harking back to an earlier time - and let's face it, one that most of us perceive as and can almost always agree is better than the way things are today (even if our rose-tinted spectacles trick us, and sometimes they were not).

When Better Homes and Gardens Real Estate posted a black and white photo of a well-kept house with the John Ed Pearce quote *"Home is a place you grow up wanting to leave, and grow old wanting to go back to,"* (http://bit.ly/betterhomesviral) it received over 2,000 likes, 675 shares, and 30 comments within a period of a few days. For a Facebook Page whose posts normally receive significantly less engagement, this example - watermarked with the company's branding - was a real success in helping to grow brand awareness. It perfectly captures the emotional ties that people have with the house they grew up in, and demonstrates the human side of the brand as well.

Humor

Since - for the vast majority of people - social media is a place to connect with friends and family in a relaxed and casual manner, humorous graphics make for a really effective strategy for driving engagement and interest in your brand. In the following example, *Dove* uses humor to promote a web series that is designed to encourage conversation around the topic of body image anxiety. An image of a man's head is accompanied by two cartoon-like bubbles. The first, underneath a "THINKS" banner reads, *"Witty, caring and so clever! You make me the proudest dad on earth!"* The second, underneath a "SAYS" title reads *"You look nice dear."* The image is accompanied by the caption, *"Sometimes it's hard for dads to express what they're really feeling. Help him say it in a way that will boost your daughter's confidence. http://selfesteem.dove.com/"* In this example, humor is used as a way to make a somewhat serious topic less intimidating for *Dove*'s fans; it touches on something that many of its customers will relate to, and makes them feel like *Dove* understands them: http://bit.ly/dovehumor

Of course, your use of humor needn't be connected to something as serious as the last example - anything that tickles the funny bones of your audience is a good way to establish and build a closer relationship with them. In the following example, *General Electric* uses a graphic to tell a silly joke, with a play on words: *"Lightning never makes a good party guest. It doesn't know how to conduct itself,"* along with the text caption *"This shouldn't come as a shock."* http://bit.ly/genelecjoke1

All that said, the more relatable you make the humor to your brand and the interests of your fans, and the experiences they encounter in real-life, the better. To imagine an obvious example, a funny photo about the perils of running out of coffee at the office would probably not do very well on a Facebook Page dedicated to a brand that sells exotic fruit teas.

Facts, figures, and being valuable

Not everybody is impressed by complicated mathematics and technical information, but most people *do* love a juicy fact or mind-boggling statistic - something that makes them say "wow" and want to pass it on to a friend. Think about all the amazing facts and trivia related to your brand and industry (the total number of hours involved in bringing a big project to life, the amazing weight of pasta consumed at your restaurant in a week, etc.) and feed that out to your audience in powerful image posts that will create a positive emotional response that they will associate with your brand. In the following example, Animal Planet India posts a photo of a bald eagle in full flight, along with the text overlay, "Did you know? Bald eagles can climb up to 300m in the air." http://bit.ly/apifact. Alternatively - as with photographs - graphics can be made to share valuable snippets of information. In the following example, outdoor living brand, L.L. Bean, helps fans spruce up their knowledge of common camping symbols (http://bit.ly/llbeancamping).

Company announcements

Sometimes *showing* people can be better than spelling things out in words, and this is certainly the case where announcements on social media are concerned. Whether it be the launch of a new product, the start of a seasonal promotion, or just a great big thank you to your fans for helping to reach a milestone like 25 years in business, a graphic is a really good way to exude your brand personality to do this. In the following example, *Salesforce* posts a branded image to Twitter in order to celebrate 15 years in business. The text overlay reads *"Thank you for 15 awesome years together,"* and is accompanied with a text update that reads *"Today Salesforce turns 15! Many thanks to our customers, employees, partners, and community"*. Updates like this help to make customers feel appreciated by the companies that they support, therein strengthening the relationship between both parties: http://bit.ly/salesforcethanks

Product annotations

If your product or service has special features that deserve to be shown off, then annotating your images to highlight these details is a tactic worth considering, especially as they might get overlooked in a text caption. The following example from *McDonald's* in the UK is a satirical take on this approach, but I chose it because it demonstrates how the concept *could* work well for more sensible situations. The post in question is an image of "The Left-Handed Big Mac" burger, complete with annotations to show off its "ergonomically designed bun for left-inclined grip," "100% beef patty rotated 180% left to maximize control and stability," and "Special Sauce redistributed to improve balance." In a world where this example *was* serious, I would also give it credit for the way that the amount of text is not over-done (three short bullet points; very readable), and for the way it simply and clearly demonstrate the product's hidden benefits: http://bit.ly/lefthandedburger

Fun and games

As mentioned previously, many people treat social media as a time to relax, unwind and have some fun. Your brand can be a part of this through the use of images that act as a trivia question, spot the difference, a word search, etc. Content like this shows off your brand's light-hearted side, and the challenges you set will drive engagement from your audiences, as well as offering a subtle marketing opportunity. In the following example, Fair Trade Certified posts a Fair Trade Word Search as an image to their Facebook Page, along with a text caption that reads: *"Here's a fun challenge to kick off your Monday! Press 'like' if you found 3 Fair Trade products in less than 10 seconds!"* http://bit.ly/ftwordsearch

5 Easy Ways to Create Irresistible Photos and Graphics for Social Media

Creating professional-looking graphics for social media needn't be a massive time suck, and you won't be required to have expert photo-editing skills to furnish something that is incredibly share-worthy either. Of course, if you are a Photoshop or Illustrator whizz, then that'll give you the most flexibility possible, but if you're not, here are a selection of my go-to tools for pumping out top notch graphics with little time and effort required:

Picmonkey

PicMonkey (http://www.picmonkey.com) is the perfect online tool for creating social media graphics in no time at all - just choose a photo from a Facebook or other web account, or upload one to edit. Once you're set, you'll have options to crop, rotate, add filters, resize, sharpen, choose frames, and lots more - all for free. Premium options are annotated with a little orange crown, but you can still produce some really great results without them.

Canva

Canva (http://www.canva.com) is widely recommended by social media pros as a must-visit destination for creating social media and blog graphics, as well as cover photos, image collages, and posters. Although you can upload and edit your own images for free, the tool also offers a search engine that will pull in thousands of stock photos priced at as little as $1.00 each, for you to use in your graphics and edit as you please.

Fotor

Fotor (http://www.fotor.com/) is an increasingly popular solution for swift social media graphic creation, not least because of its huge selection of fonts - lifted both from your computer, and online. You'll also find plenty one one-click options for photo editing, including image cropping, rotation, borders, and more.

PowerPoint

If you'd prefer more control over your social media graphic creation, Microsoft's PowerPoint (or Apple's Keynote) make surprisingly versatile tools for this task - and of course, they're super simple to use, with easy-to-add text and image effects. Simply create your image and choose to save the slide as an image for use on social media.

Mobile apps

For social media graphic creation when you're on the move, there is a huge selection of apps available to choose from, both free and paid. Some of my favorite image editing and text-overlay apps, available include VSCO Cam (http://vsco.co/vscocam, iOS and Android), Shark Photo Editor (iOS and Android), Over (iOS), and Phonto (iOS and Android).

Infographics on Social Media: How to Create Irresistible Visualisations for Ideas and Data

As the amount of information we are bombarded with daily has exploded in the age of the Internet, so too has the use of infographics as a way to help people digest data and knowledge in a quick and efficient way. Infographics combine the best elements of text, images, and design to create a "visual shorthand" in a way that is attractive, shareable, and has the potential to go viral. The best infographics exude an emotional influence that prompts viewers to read them from top to bottom, then pass the information onto others.

While an infographic's primary function may be to re-purpose a complex idea in a much more palatable manner, it has other positive side effects like positioning you as an authority figure on a subject, increasing brand awareness, and driving traffic to your website. Nowadays, the sheer amount of infographics being published means that yours needs to do more than look pretty if you are going to seize the opportunity to engage (and benefit from) the audience that sees it. The best infographics are helpful and thought-provoking - not simply a list of big statistics combined with pretty clipart.

With all of the above in mind, what follows is a number of ways to plan for creating top quality infographics. When you read these strategies, consider the fact that a great many infographic ideas will have already been covered. In order to stand out from the crowd, ask yourself if you can present an idea in a more unique, updated, and interesting way: something that will really benefit your target audience and ensure that your brand name isn't simply slapped onto the bottom of a visualization that will be lost in the crowd.

Have a clear focus

Infographics work best when the topic it covers is laser-targeted; don't attempt to cover too wide a spectrum of information or you risk losing your audience before you even get going. When you've nailed down on a particular topic and have fully researched the idea, take a close look at data you have compiled and remove all of the extraneous details. When a viewer sees an infographic, you want to tell them just what they need to understand the message behind it, without any of the unnecessary fluff. It's a tricky balance because you want to give people a sense of all of the information that is available and context for it, but not so much that they are overwhelmed. When all of your infographic's data is laid out, viewers should be able to see the bigger picture naturally emerging as they read through it.

Note: On the subject of focus, no good infographic is complete without an attention-grabbing headline - something short, strong (and even emotionally-driven) that will tell people exactly what the infographic entails, and encourage people to keep reading. Some of the most widely used infographic-headline conventions mirror those of blog post titles, e.g. questions (*Is It Too Late to Stop Global Warming?*), numbered lists (*15 Stunning Facts You Didn't Know About Thimbles*), and the promise of quick, useful knowledge (*The Fisherman's Ultimate Cheat Sheet*).

Solve a problem

One of the primary purposes people use the web for is answers to questions, and infographics can be a very good way to formulate knowledge and advice in a compelling manner. People often don't have the time (or just don't want to) read through a lot of text in order to learn how to fix whatever it is that needs fixing, so in this respect, an infographic is the perfect way to lay out the issue and provide a solution in an easily-digested way. Embedded as part of a longer blog post that *does* spell out the problem at hand, along with a much more detailed explanation of how to overcome it, infographics gives readers options about how they would like to proceed, as well as acting as a hugely shareable piece of visual content.

To prove that infographics work for almost any subject, let's take the question "*How do I make a compost pile?*" In the following infographic called *"How to Compost"* by PBS (http://bit.ly/makecompost) tells us what composting is, and - in six simple steps with illustrations - shows us how anybody can start making and managing their own compost area.

Simplify a complex idea

In the next example, Door to Door Organics takes a huge and complex subject - the problem of food waste around the world - then uses an infographic to simplify the major talking points, and make the subject much easier for viewers to understand (http://bit.ly/foodwasteinfographic). The visual starts by introducing the problem (1.3 billion tons of all edible food produced worldwide is wasted or lost each year), and then breaks it down into smaller sub-sections that are anchored by questions: "Why is this a problem?" and "What can you do about it?" Whatever idea you want to visually represent (tackling a huge societal or cultural idea like global food waste, picking apart the complexities of your product designs, explaining the history of the culture of your business, etc.), an infographic can help you do this in a simplified, structured, and visually stimulating way that your audience will enjoy.

Note: If your infographic has been built to advertise a product or service, focus less on self-promotion and more on the *story* element: of course, tell people about the features and the data, but also communicate how and why they came to exist. Infographics that are, for all intents and purposes, blatant adverts, are not very appealing, do not connect emotionally with audiences, and therefore are unlikely to be read for long or shared onwards.

Make it newsworthy

Building on the point of making ideas easier for your audience to understand through the medium of infographics, one of the best ways to take advantage of this is to capitalize on breaking news and trending topics within your industry. When news has recently broken and not fully filtered into the public consciousness, *you* can become the source that helps them to get a firm grasp on what is happening. Finding newsworthy infographic ideas is as simple as keeping an eye on the current events that matter to you and your audience, whether that be through news websites, RSS feeds, or discussions on Reddit and Internet message boards. In the following example, the Garden Media Group published an infographic that covers the top garden trends of 2014, featuring topics such as composting, super foods, and bees (any of which - as we've seen in the case of compositing - could exist as infographics in their own right): http://bit.ly/gardentrends14

Don't lose your personality

If your infographic deals with a lot of data, a serious subject matter, or you are concentrating hard on simply making the visualisation and its ideas clear, it can be easy to let the personality of your brand falter, and to give the impression to your audience that you do not see passion or enjoyment in what you do. Work just as hard on your copy as you do your images, and remember, especially, that humor is a very effective way to open people up to ideas.

Note: On the subject of copy, try your best not to make an infographic the visual representation of a blog post. Keep the language you use simple and tight, and find the best balance between words and images.

Brand your infographic effectively

I touched on this very briefly above, but it is *so* important that your infographic is branded effectively - after all, the eventual purpose of all the effort you put in is to get people interested in who you are and what you do - and how are they ever going to do that if you don't tell them? Add your company name, logo, and website to the top and bottom of your infographic so that people know who was behind it, even if it is widely shared around without proper accreditation. The added benefit of this, too, is that no unscrupulous individual can post your infographic to their blog or website and take credit for it.

Use reliable sources of data

Most data or fact-heavy infographics are supported by a list of sources, normally tucked away at the bottom of the image. It is *so* important that the data you feature in your infographic is reliable and accurate, otherwise you could have the prettiest design going but it won't matter as your credibility will take a huge hit. The best way to ensure that you have the most fool-proof data is to gather it from up-to-date and official sources - don't rely on second-hand information gathered by others, always track it back to the original researcher. If you're not having much luck doing the research on your own, it might be time - if the funds are available - to hire a professional to find and provide a concrete data set for you. If you decide on this route, ensure that you give a detailed outline of the infographic topic and the kind of data you want them to track down.

4 Easy and Free Ways to Create Infographics for Social Media

Although sometimes it might seem that the creation of an infographic simply involves summarizing a blog post and adding a few images (and many people do!), the best examples out there will have taken many hours to finish, with every small design detail poured over to the nth degree. With time, budget, and skill a limiting factor for many marketers, the tools below are "quick and dirty" ways to create infographics that remain professional-looking and are much more share-worthy. With that said, these are just a few very basic guidelines that you'll want to follow if you don't want the results of your work to end up looking terrible:

- Infographics can be designed to any vertical length, but you don't want to make one that is *so* long that it deters readers from wanting to read it from start to finish. According to research carried out by KISSmetrics, to be optimized for reading and most shareable, an infographic shouldn't cover more than 6 main points[7]. If your topic needs more than six main points to cover in full, split the infographic into a series and make sure your audience knows this is the case. As for physical size, I'd recommend somewhere around the 8,000 pixels mark as a maximum limit.

- Structurally, you will want to design an infographic that has a logical flow from top to bottom, drawing the readers' eye from one section of the visual's narrative to the next. If it helps, sketch out a wireframe of the design before you dive into making the full graphics. As most people will scan (rather than fully read) your infographic, make sure that the most important points are highlighted, either by text size or color. Keep the number of fonts you use down to a minimum (two is good), and make sure that they are readable both as headlines, sub-headlines, and ordinary text.

- As for the graphics and images you use, implement a style

(complete with high resolution illustrations or vectors, i.e. no pixelated images!) that matches the overall tone of your infographic's topic, and pair it with an appropriate color scheme - use Kuler or Color Scheme Designer to create your palette.

With the basics out the way, here is a selection of free online infographic-building, tools.

Easel.ly

My personal favorite, Easel.ly (http://easel.ly) allows you to instantly create infographics, offers a dozen or so free templates to get you off on the right track, and has a library full of fonts, shapes, backgrounds, arrows, and connector lines that you can customize. Simply drag and drop objects as you wish, and even upload your own images to compliment the web app's own. When you're done, there are options to download your finished infographic in low or high quality, and as a PDF.

Piktochart

Like Easel.ly, Picktochart (http://piktochart.com/ allows you to choose from a select number of templates and themes to create a free infographic. With a paid account, you'll get full access to its graphics library, and be able to download your finished work in high resolution.

Venngage

Another drag-and-drop infographic creation tool, Venngage (https://venngage.com/) provides free users with a generous selection of templates, as well as a variety of drag-and-drop tools that allow you to customize your creation with relative ease. Sadly, if you want to download your image, use the full library of themes and templates, and access a variety of other perks, you'll have to cough up money for the privilege.

Infogr.am

Unlike the above, Infogr.am (https://infogr.am) has a focus that is slightly more data-heavy. The free version allows you to create lovely-looking graphs from a limited set of templates, which can then be shared via a custom infogr.am link. Pro accounts allow you to download your

creation, instantly share to social media, remove the site's watermark, and more.

Where to find vector images for infographics

Infographics are often laden with beautifully bold and colorful vector images rather than photographs. If you don't have an artist to create your own vectors or the sites above to not offer what you need, consider portals like Vector Stock (http://www.vectorstock.com) for affordable graphics, or Freepik (http:///www.freepik.com) for thousands of vectors for the princely sum of zero.

Animated GIFs on Social Media: Best Practices and Strategies for Success

The GIF image format - and animated GIFs in particular - have been around for a *long* time, but the latter's popularity has surged in an era of faster Internet speeds, social media, and the invention of micro-blogging sites like Tumblr. The animated GIF's small size (both physically and data-wise) makes it a useful marketing tool for a number of reasons, and normally exists in one of three forms: using multiple still images to create an ever-repeating "slideshow," lifting a snippet from a video that you own, or lifting a section of video from a recording found online. Let's take a look at some of the most common ways animated GIFs are used in social media marketing, and how you might want to use them too:

Expressing a thought or emotion

Perhaps the most frequent reason for the use of animated GIFs is to express a thought or emotion, or hammer home a statement or opinion, in a much more dynamic manner than a static image or emoticon could do on its own. The key to this strategy is choosing the right GIF to use: a humorous animation is often the type that is best received, but if the one you pick doesn't fit well with your thought or statement, then the whole idea will fall flat on its face. Buzzfeed's writers are masters of matching written words with appropriate (and often funny) animated GIFs. A visit to its website will provide you with hundreds of articles full of examples, but here is just a very short selection:

- *19 Reasons Summer In The City is Terrible And Wants to Hurt You*: http://www.buzzfeed.com/lukebailey/sod-off-sun
- *17 Things You Didn't Know About McDonald's:* http://www.buzzfeed.com/jessicamisener/things-you-didnt-know-about-mcdonalds
- *28 Things People Who Can't Sleep Will Totally Understand:* http://www.buzzfeed.com/javim2/28-things-people-who-cant-sleep-will-totally-unde-bw9q

As you'll no doubt notice, a significant portion of Buzzfeed's articles are simple numbered lists. Not only are these perfectly suited to the implementation of animated GIFs in blog posts (one GIF per each one-sentence point), but they are very quick to read, and, therefore, much more shareable than they might otherwise be, especially when posted to social media. Here's another good example of a "reaction GIF," courtesy of Soccer.com: http://bit.ly/soccergif - its reaction to the roll out of animated GIF compatibility for Twitter.

Showcasing a product or service

When you want to show off a product or process, sometimes a static image just won't do the job as satisfactorily as you like. While a short video *would* do the trick, sometimes an animated GIF (instantly playing and repeating over and over) is a better option. This works whether you want to show an assortment of products in one animation, compare two products side by side, or give a quick demonstration about how something works. In the following GIF, the Huffington Post uses an animated GIF on Pinterest to demonstrate how to effectively use a foam roller: http://bit.ly/pinfoamroller. And here, Kitchen Tips and Tricks demonstrates a quick way to peel potatoes: http://bit.ly/peelpots

Announcements and call to actions

One of the biggest uses of animated GIFs (especially in web banner ads) is as a way to catch peoples' eyes and encourage them to click through to see your content - a product launch, a special offer, etc. Despite its prevalent use in web ads, I have no objections to it appearing as social media content as long as the strategy is used sparingly. Knowing how much ads on the web are despised, you have to be careful to ensure that your brand's self-promotion on social media isn't dragged down into the same category. One company that takes good advantage of the brevity and usefulness of GIFs is the English fashion brand, Burberry. Across Pinterest and Twitter, it uses the medium to highlight products and show behind the scenes at its catwalk shows, and make announcements. In the following example, it invites fans to watch one of its London fashion shows with a classy animated GIF used to show off an invitation card: http://bit.ly/burberryinvite

Reliving a scene or a moment

Another simple and effective way to use animated GIFs is to tell the story of a moment in time: it could be a replay of something unexpected, funny, or cool that happened at an event you were attending or showing a sped-up progression of how you remodeled your store, for example. When you record videos, ask yourself what the most "GIF-worthy" moment of it is, then use this to create an animation to share on social media that will encourage people to click and watch the footage in full (for added context and higher quality), or simply pass on to their friends - added exposure for your brand.

Just a cool visual effect

As the animated GIF format sees snippets of video repeat over and over, this can be used to create some cool effects - in particular, the seamless loop. Check out this example from Wendy's, which combines humor and a seamless loop to create a mesmerizing, shareable, visual effect: http://bit.ly/wendysgif. Although Wendy's example is computer generated, the same effect can be achieved in real life, as long as the frame at the beginning and end of the clip you want to use as an animated GIF are almost identical, so viewers cannot tell where it starts and where it ends. For all kinds of inspiration, check out the Perfect Loops subreddit on Reddit (http://www.reddit.com/r/perfectLoops) and consider using a tool like Loop Findr (http://loopfindr.tumblr.com/), which automatically finds the best spot in a video clip to create a seamless loop.

4 Easy Ways to Find And Create Animated GIFS For Social Media

"Back in the day," a layman wanting to find or create a GIF was pretty much stuck without the tools and technical knowhow needed to create one from scratch. These days, however, there are a myriad of GIF search engines and creation tools, both for computers and mobile devices.

Giphy

Described by its creator as *"the largest GIF search engine in the known galaxy,"*[8] Giphy (http://www.giphy.com) is the Google of the animated GIF world, and my recommended go-to site for tracking down already-existing GIFs for use in your blog posts and social media content. Its content is categorized in detail to help you find the most suitable content as quickly as possible, and when you do find the perfect GIF, you'll be presented with numerous options to help you present it as you wish: a share to social networks, a direct link, embed codes, and more. Don't forget to grab the GIF's source URL so that you can credit it correctly.

MakeAGIF

Arguably the best animated GIF maker on the web, MakeAGiF (http://makeagif.com/) allows you to stitch together still images, upload video clips, or grab sections from content hosted on YouTube. Make sure to sign up for an account so that the result doesn't include a watermark, and so that the size of the resulting GIF is larger than that for non-registered users.

Jiffy

Jiffy (http://bit.ly/jiffychrome) is an extension for the Google Chrome web browser. Once installed, a new setting will appear on YouTube video pages that will allow you to convert a portion of the clip into an animated GIF. Once the conversion is complete, you simply download the image from the link provided.

Moquu and GIF Camera

Preferring to dub itself as an "animated photo" tool, Moquu (http://www.moqu.us/) for iOS allows you to import or shoot photos or video clips that are then converted into animated GIFs to be shared wherever you choose. The Android app, GIF Camera (http://bit.ly/gifcameraandroid), works with a similar premise - a simple and unfussy photo-or-video-to-GIF maker that is super handy to have ready when you're on the go.

Adobe Photoshop or GIMP

For pros and control freaks alike, using software like Adobe Photoshop (paid) or GIMP (free) is the recommended method for creating and editing animated GIFs on a frame-by-frame basis. Check out the following tutorial for instructions of how to create animated GIFs in Photoshop (http://bit.ly/animatedgifphotoshop) and GIMP (http://bit.ly/animatedgifgimp).

Memes on Social Media: Best Practices and Strategies for Success

The word "meme" originally comes from the 1976 book, The Selfish Gene, by evolutionary biologist, Richard Dawkins, where the term is defined as a unit of cultural knowledge that is passed between people. In modern terms, Social Fresh says *"a meme is a categorization of a cultural trend or truth, a unit for communicating and collectively sharing cultural ideas through words, symbols and pictures."*[9] In simpler terms - and in the majority of cases - they are funny, entertaining, relatable, and creative images (combined with text) that have huge viral potential. From "Bad Luck Brian" to "First World Problems" and the "Socially Awkward Penguin," memes are everywhere on social media, and - used effectively - can become a key ingredient in any brand's social media marketing mix. Despite memes' proliferation online, they are not always judged upon as being the most "high quality" pieces of content. As a result, you must carefully consider their use as part of your strategy, based on several important factors. Let's look at some of the most important considerations for creating and choosing great memes:

Understand the concept

Memes become popular because they are easily digested and extremely shareable. If you're the type of individual or brand that doesn't closely follow online culture and are not quite sure what a popular meme looks like and how they work, it is important that you learn to do so before diving in. As mentioned above, memes are largely light-hearted and whimsical in nature, and rarely used to promote a serious message. The most common layout of a meme is two short lines of text laid out like a one-liner joke: first the setup, then the punch line. Take some time to study some popular and successful examples of memes so that you can best position yourself to make the biggest impact when you begin to share others' or create your own - you'll find lots of good examples at the websites mentioned throughout this chapter.

Make it relevant

With hundreds (if not thousands) of different meme categories to choose from, it is important that the ones you select are relevant to your audience and your brand. One good acid test is the following: if you have to explain the concept of a meme to your audience when you post it, it probably isn't going to resonate with them. Alternatively, *listen* to your audience and let them do the work for you. If they are already fervently sharing a meme, then hop on that bandwagon and share it too - especially if you can put your own unique spin on the subject matter. Examples of brands that have successfully tied memes to their own marketing include Virgin's use of "Success Kid" (http://bit.ly/successkidvirgin) and Mosquito Magnet's use of Somecards' sarcastic postcards (http://bit.ly/mosquitosomecard).

Don't miss the boat

Like so much of pop culture content, the majority of memes are fads - here today and gone tomorrow. Ideally, you want to latch onto the popularity of a meme while it is still in the early stages of its popularity, positioning your brand as "in the know" and a trendsetter. By the time a meme's popularity has reached saturation point, your use of it becomes less and less effective. The website Know Your Meme (http://knowyourmeme.com/) is an incredibly useful resource for keeping tabs on the emergence of new and trending memes, complete with a full history and explanation of each. My go-to source, however, is Reddit - specifically the Advice Animals subreddit (http://www.reddit.com/r/adviceanimals). If a category of meme is trending, chances are you'll find it on the first few pages here. You might not necessarily find an already-posted meme with text that works exactly for your brand, but you're sure to find an example that you can use for inspiration to create your own.

Move on quickly

Nothing demonstrates your lack of cutting edge than if you continue to use a meme that has long fallen out of popular use. As soon as one meme falls by the wayside, another one is guaranteed to replace it, so make sure that your meme of choice isn't already in steep decline. One way to do this is to check on its search interest via Google Trends (handily, this data is displayed at the bottom of every meme explanation entry on Know Your Meme (http://knowyourmeme.com/). One glance at the chart will tell you if the meme's popularity is continuing to rise, or very much on the wane.

2 Quick and Easy Ways to Create Memes for Social Media

Unlike photos, graphics, and infographics, creating or finding an effective meme can, in many cases, take just a matter of seconds. Let's take a look at some of the best options available:

imgur

imgur's Meme Generator (http://imgur.com/memegen) is arguably the most popular meme creator online. You'll be presented with a list of the current most popular memes to edit with your own text, or you can select one of dozens from a drop-down list. If you're in the business of creating your own memes, there's even an option to upload a new background image. Whichever option you choose, finishing up your masterpiece is as simple as typing your text into the template (click and drag to change the position and size of the text if required) and clicking the "make this meme!" button. You'll then be able to save your finished meme in a variety of sizes, share it direct to numerous social media sites, or grab a code to embed it onto your website.

Apps for iOS and Android

imgur's mobile website is just as effective as the desktop version for meme generation, but if you're low on data or without a connection when inspiration strikes, you'll want an app to be there for you. There are numerous meme creation apps available, but my favorites are *Meme Generator by Meme Crunch* for iOS and *Meme Generator Free* for Android. Both allow you to quickly and easily select and design dozens of memes on the move, then share them onto social networks or save them to your device for later There's sections for New and Popular memes, too, and like imgur, an option to upload and design your own custom viral image.

Presentations on Social Media: Best Practices and Strategies for Success

If, a few years ago, you asked me what entered into my head when I thought of the word "presentation," I'd have said it was the image of someone droning on for hours in front of a terrible collection of PowerPoint slides made up of terrible clip art and way too much text. In many respects, that scenario is *still* happening the world over, but in the social media marketing sphere, things have moved on considerably. No longer limited to a mishmash of ugly CD-based clipart and a paltry selection of fonts *and* coupled with an environment where the hunger for quick, informative, and visual content is insatiable, presentations - done right - can be an incredibly powerful and shareable part of your social media marketing strategy.

Central to the popularity of presentations in the social media age is Slideshare, the world's largest community for sharing slideshow presentations. With over 60 million monthly visitors and 215 million page views as of Q4 2013, it is one of the most visited websites in the world and *hugely* popular with professionals. Created in familiar programs like PowerPoint and Keynote, presentations uploaded to Slideshare can be viewed on your profile, embedded on your website, or shared to social networks. Let's look at some of the key strategies you should employ to make the most of what Slideshare has to offer:

Ideas for Slideshare presentations

The most popular use of Slideshare is for businesses to share their knowledge and expertise; a way to encourage discussion around topics, build authority and generate leads by driving interest in what the company in question offers.

Share information and advice

Some of the most popular types of presentations on Slideshare reflect those that are similarly successful in the blogging world - helpful, insightful, and educational content, often presented as a numbered list. Glancing at the site's most-viewed presentations on the day of writing this, topics include "North America's 50 Most In-Demand Employers ", "20 Event Planning Fails Your Guests Hate," and "10 Key Ingredients in Creating and Telling a Story."

Other, non-numbered examples include "How to Give Effective Feedback to Employees," "The Future of the Customer Relationship." and "How to Never Run Out of Great Ideas" (http://bit.ly/greatideaspresentation).In general, honing in on one specific topic works better than trying to cover several. If you have lots to say, try splitting the presentations up into different parts based on sub-categories of information.

Show off data and information

As well as traditional PowerPoint-style presentations, infographics are very much encouraged on Slideshare. In July 2013, the site even rolled out an infographic-specific player, which will automatically be applied to a creation when it is uploaded. And if your infographic is embedded from Slideshare, it will display in its entirety - no scrolling required. In a study of over 1,000 infographics, Slideshare found that they are liked 4x more than ordinary presentations, and 23x more than documents, so they're definitely worth publishing to your account. Check out this example of an infographic entitled *Small Business Big Impact: 10 Facts About Small Businesses* (http://bit.ly/smallbizbigimpact)

Note: Infographics uploaded to Slideshare need to be saved in a one-page PDF format in order to be detected.

Re-purpose existing content

One great opportunity with Slideshare is how it can host existing content from other sources (such as evergreen blog posts) and re-purpose them as a visual project for a whole new audience of viewers. Whether your goal is to convert *every* blog post you write into a Slideshare presentation (or just the ones that prove most popular), there's no denying the extra mileage that you can give to them.

Tease content and drive viewers to your website

Say you created a presentation called '25 Ways to Make the Most of eBay'. Instead of uploading a presentation that contains all 25 tips, only upload 15 of them. Then, in the last slide of your show, include a call to action: a link to send them to your blog or website that has published the list in its entirety. This strategy can be really beneficial, especially if the presentation in question becomes popular and generates lots of views, and is a good way of leveraging the huge audience on Slideshare to boost your external efforts.

Need inspiration?

If your imagination needs a spark for a Slideshare presentation idea, look no further than what is already proving popular. Check out the Popular and Featured sections of the site for a selection some of the best and most imaginative slideshows. Mirror their styles, but ensure you have a point of difference that makes your work even better than what is currently available.

7 Ways to Build and Optimize Presentations for Social Media

Be highly visual and limit the amount of text

In a book all about visual imagery, this one is obvious - but if your presentation is just a converted blog post, viewers will not be attracted to it. As the old saying goes, a picture tells a thousand words, so use the power of visuals and metaphors to hammer your points home. Scour the web for high quality images to make your slideshows as professional as possible. On top of that, stick to a consistent look and feel, so that your content is easily identifiable if you decide to upload regularly.

When your slideshows are highly visual, naturally this will leave less space for text – but, in a sense, this is what you want. A good rule of thumb is to give each slide just one point or snippet of information to caption an image *or* have an image on its own on a slide, and text to explain it on the next. These strategies ensure that people can progress through them quickly, maintaining their interest throughout - no one wants to encounter and digest ten long bullet points per slide! This approach also makes sense because your audience will not have a speaker to guide them through the presentation, so the aim is to make it super easy for them to consume, whilst being stimulating and engaging throughout.

Optimize your title slide

All captivating Slideshare presentations have one thing in common - an awesome first, title slide. It's the first thing that potential viewers will see of your work, so make it work for you like you would a video thumbnail on YouTube, with bold colors, eye-catching videos, a font that can be read at small sizes in search results (and when you get featured on the Slideshare home page ;)) and a title that will encourage people click to see more.

Add a captivating title, a compelling description, and relevant tags

Ensure your presentation's title is simple and keyword-rich so that you give your work the best chance of being found both in Slideshare and Google search. The latter point applies to the description, which is also important to search engine optimization. In addition to describing what your presentation is about, add your contact details - web address, physical address, telephone number - into your presentation's description so that customers have an easy way to find you after being wowed by your work. In order to help your presentation be found in the site's search engine, be sure to add a selection of relevant tags as well.

Fill in your presentation notes

When you add extra notes to your presentation, they will appear underneath your Slideshare content once it is uploaded to the website. Not only does this provide extra value to readers who want to delve deeper into the information that you are providing, but it can also benefit from a search engine optimization standpoint, as they will pick up on this additional, keyword-rich text.

Optimum presentation length and a call to action

There is an argument that shorter presentations work best at engaging an audience, but given Slideshare's largely professional audience, an argument is emerging for the opposite. I would suggest experimenting with different lengths of presentations (i.e. 10-15 slides one time, and up to 60 or so for another) to see what works best for you. Maybe you'll grab a more casual audience when your presentations are shorter, but pull in the more professional viewers when your content is longer and more detailed. Whatever the length of your slideshow, add in a call to action encouraging your viewers to act upon the information they have just seen. Do you want them to call you, email, check out your Facebook Page, visit your online store, etc? State the case clearly for them, and hyperlink the text to encourage click-throughs.

Note: If you are a Slideshare Pro member, the site will allow you to embed email opt-in forms into your presentations. Placed at the end of the deck (rather than the beginning which can come across as pushy), they can be very effective in attracting impressed viewers to sign up to your newsletter, webinar, etc.

Don't bother with animations, upload as pdf

Content uploaded to Slideshare will be converted for presentation, and part of this means that animations created in programs such as Microsoft PowerPoint will not show. The best way to ensure the integrity of your work as it journeys from your hard drive to the web is to save it in PDF format for uploads to SlideShare.

Embedding and sharing strategy

Slideshare presentations are easily embedded (simply grab the code from the presentation page), so make a feature of them in a blog post, an email newsletter, or as interactive content for Twitter and LinkedIn - Slideshare presentations play directly within the news feeds of these two social networks. When embedding your presentation, click the 'Customize' button; make sure to check the 'Without related content' box, to make sure no one who views it on your website or blog is distracted by competing Slideshare shows. Users of Slideshare will also be able to embed your work too, which can often exponentially expand the exposure of your presentations, and vastly increase the amount of reviews it receives.

Images on Facebook: Statistics, Case Studies, and Best Practices

Best for: photographs, graphics, memes, collages, and user-generated content.

Images on Facebook: the stats

In the western world, Facebook is the grand daddy of all social networks. With over a billion active users on desktop and mobiles, it has allowed individuals to connect with their friends, and brands - through Facebook Pages - to build relationships with their audience - in a way that had never been seen before. As the site has developed and grown over the years since its launch in 2004, there has been an ever-greater emphasis on making News Feeds and Pages more visually compelling, in tandem with the types of content that its users like to post. This shift can be seen in the larger screen real estate given to image uploads and galleries, photos attached to linked blog posts, News Feed and side bar advertising, and even the introduction of auto-playing videos.

In April 2014, the social media analytics company, Social Bakers, released findings from a study on the most popular types of Facebook posts published by over 30,000 different brands between February 24th and March 24th 2014, and the interaction that these posts garnered. It discovered that *most* of the content brands post to Facebook included photos - 75% of all content in the one-month period. The next most popular posts were link shares (10%) and text updates (6%). When examining the engagement that each of these types of post received, the dominance of photos was even more pronounced. This observation was true whether the Facebook Page had a huge audience (over 1,000,000 fans), a medium sized audience (between 100,000 and 999,999 fans) or a smaller audience (between 1 and 99,000 fans). In singling out the most-engaged-with 10% of posts made by the 30,000 Pages that were analyzed, photo posts made up a whopping 87% of those posts. Interestingly, videos and albums achieved almost the same share of total interactions as they did overall share of published content - around 3-4%. [10]

Images on Facebook: A case study

In the run up to Mother's Day in 2012, 1-800-Flowers.com posted a gallery of images on its Facebook Page depicting a variety of styles of bouquets, and asked moms to choose which one they would most like to receive for Mother's Day. The four most-liked products in the campaign turned out to be four out of the five most popular bouquets for the season. The Mother's Day campaign increased engagement with 1-800-Flowers.com's wall posts by 393 percent. [11] Also key to the company's strategy is encouraging its fans to post images that feature their products, and to share the story that surrounds it. It then re-publishes these photos on its Page and uses them in Facebook advertising to send a strong message about how much its customers love the brand. 1-800 Flowers's mission is to deliver smiles to people, and are constantly surprised by how much their fans love to share these smiles to their friends and family on Facebook.

Images on Facebook: best practices

- Facebook cover photos are 851 x 315 pixels. Use yours in an impactful and imaginative way to represent your brand, and appeal to new and existing fans alike.

- When uploading an image to the Facebook timeline, a thumbnail is generated automatically to fit within a box that is 504px by 504px. In order to take maximum advantage of this space, upload a square photo that is at least 504px wide (landscape photos will be scaled to 540 pixels wide, portrait photos will be scaled to 504 pixels high and centered with a grey bar on each side).

- When uploading multiple images, the first one to appear in the upload dialog box will always display first, and sometimes appear bigger than those next to it. Always drag the "primary" image to the left-most position.

- Do not upload infographics as one large, single image - they will appear crazily zoomed out and plain terrible! Instead, cut out the title or an interesting section and post this with a link and call to action that points to where the infographic is hosted in a much easier-to-digest way, e.g. on your blog or Pinterest profile.

- Since buying out Instagram in 2013, Facebook loves it when photos from the app are shared to the site, and often gives prevalence to them over images uploaded directly to your

Timeline. So, if you're using Instagram as part of your visual marketing strategy, be sure to re-purpose the content into the mix on Facebook.

For a much more wealthy and detailed outline of Facebook strategy for business, read the Facebook Tips chapter of my #1 Amazon Web Marketing Bestseller, 500 Social Media Marketing Tips.

Images on Twitter: Statistics, Case Studies, and Best Practices

Best for: photographs, infographics, user-generated images, presentations, and animated GIFs.

Images on Twitter: the stats

There was a period during Twitter's infancy and in the years that it was gaining popularity, that a lot of people - both individuals and brands - just didn't get what the service was all about. I mean, really, what use is a place to share text-only messages with a maximum limit of 140 characters? Since that time - and with the introduction of new features like image-sharing, video-playing, embedded tweets, and personalized profile branding, Twitter has grown to become part of the worldwide psyche. For businesses of any kind, it is the perfect platform to broadcast to and interact with customers in real-time. Simply Measured analyzed data collected by their analytics platform for Q4 2013 and found that 92 percent of companies among the Interbrand 100 post to Twitter at least once per day. [12]

Statistics show that visual content is effective on Twitter, driving more engagement on the content that brands post. A study by Buddy Media study in 2012 found that tweets with images received two times the amount of engagement with those without. [13] When you consider that this data was gathered at a time before images uploaded to Twitter were integrated into the news feed (as they are now), it really reflect the influence that visual storytelling can have on the platform. In a more recent study, Simply Measured crunched numbers from its social media analytics platform for the final quarter of 2013, finding that tweets that include photos and links receive 150 percent more engagement than brand averages.

Images on Twitter: a case study

The fashion retail chain, American Apparel, is a huge advocate of Twitter for business, and uses a lot of visual imagery to help drive engagement with its customers. In fact, the vast majority of its tweets use a combination of image, text, and links. It uses images to showcase new products or give a sneak peek at upcoming lines, show behind the scenes snaps at photo shoots and events, and more. These photos are a mix, from professional shoots to much more candid examples that reflect the platform's immediacy and relaxed tone.

For Halloween 2013, it asked fans to pick one of the costume ideas it shared to enter to win that whole costume. As a bonus, the entry method required people to enter their e-mail address via a Twitter Lead Generation Card (a sign-up form appearing direct within the Twitter feed, complete with a highly visual banner image to promote the contest and highlights its products): http://bit.ly/aahalloween

The Halloween promotion attracted with over a hundred leads (half of whom were new e-mails that did not exist in its database) and received an engagement rate of 2%. Best of all, the Twitter leads in question ordered around $90 worth of merchandise, which is about 15% higher than the brand's normal average order value. [14]

Images on Twitter: best practices

- Take advantage of Twitter's large desktop header image to showcase your brand image and personality. The ideal size for this image is of 1500 x 500 pixels.

- For neatness, images over a certain height that are uploaded to Twitter will be cropped equally from the top and bottom into a "letter box" shape. A user will have to click on the image or the "Expand" link to view it in full. Use this as an opportunity to create images that do not need expanding, or ones that *do* need expanding to reveal special offers and announcements. Use my template to help you get this design decision right every time.

- Use the half-and-half-split and "four quadrant" display of multiple image uploads to Twitter to creatively share photos collages and messages, e.g. to tell the story of an event in the life of your business, or to give a quick visual step-by-step tutorial.

- Twitter supports animated GIFs; upload them just as you would normal images, and implement them as part of your social media content and engagement strategy.

- Twitter also supports Slideshare presentations; when you link to them, they will be viewable right within users' Twitter feeds, so take advantage of this large, interactive piece of content whether it be your own, or sharing someone else's.

For a much more wealthy and detailed outline of Twitter strategy for business, read the Twitter Tips chapter of my #1 Amazon Web Marketing Bestseller, <u>500 Social Media Marketing Tips.</u>

Images on Instagram: Statistics, Case Studies, and Best Practices

Images on Instagram: the stats

There are a hundreds photo-sharing apps for mobile devices, but there is one that currently towers over all of the competition - Instagram. With a simple idea - the ability for users to instantly add vintage filters to their images (and since 2013, videos too), it has grown a large and loyal fan base of over 200 million people - it hit that number in March 2014, and had attracted over 50 million new users in the six months previous.[15] Instagram users share over 60 million photos per day, and daily engagement rates continue to rise, with some 1.6 billion "likes" given to content each and every day[16]. Other apps might offer the same functionality as Instagram (and in many cases a whole lot more), but none has captured the imagination of its audience in the same way, nor fostered a community of users for whom the app is an enormous part of their lives. It's this passionate user base that makes Instagram such a draw for brands; many have already successfully done so, with some of the devotedness that Instagram users show to the app rubbing off onto them.

Images on Instagram: case studies

Herschel Supply, famous for its backpacks that are a staple of fashion-conscious types across the world, uses Instagram to share experiences; to show fans and customers what lifestyle can be made possible as a result of using its products. [17]*"On Instagram, we're not trying to sell our products, we're trying to tell a broader story about the relationship between our audience and the places they go with their bags,"* Herschel Supply's social media and digital marketing manager, Allison Butula told Nitrogram. *"We've done this through our hashtag #WellTravelled which builds off our greater community and the images they share with us. We highlight amazing photographers that fit with our brand story and add to our narrative."* Using social media, including Instagram, Herschel Supply has achieved a 20% rise in its customer service satisfaction rate and 60% increase in overall positive brand sentiment.[18]

General Electric is one of the B2B companies taking full advantage of Instagram (http://instagram.com/generalelectric). It uses the platform as a way to tell the story of the way its work changes the world, and help people actually understand some of the many things it does. *"We do so many things, something we were looking to solve is how to explain that to people,"* Katrina Craigwell, Global Manager of Digital Marketing at General Electric told Instagram. [19] *"It's about developing an understanding for what GE does, beyond what you think it does."*

One of General Electric's primary themes is photographing big machines in a compelling way, often with an emphasis on their scale. *"Our theory was that there was a way to present our big machines in way that was beautiful, a way that people could geek out on science and technology and jet engines,"* added Craigwell.

Images on Instagram: best practices

- Do not shoot your photos within the Instagram app. Use your mobile's native camera (or any other digital camera). This gives you full control, especially if you prefer to edit your photos within a different app (to add text overlays or non-Instagram filters, for example) before importing the image into the Instagram app, adding the finishing touches, and publishing.

- Reflect the creative mindset of Instagram's culture in your portfolio - aim for quality over quantity, jump on Instagram hashtag trends, e.g. #fromwhereistand and #thingsorganizedneatly, and be very subtle with your branding.

- Be patient about getting the perfect shot; remember the guidelines we covered earlier.

- Highlight your brand culture and personality with consistent filters, color schemes, and themed content - something consistent within your gallery that distinguishes it from everyone else's.

For a much more wealthy and detailed outline of Instagram strategy for business, read the Instagram Tips chapter of my #1 Amazon Web Marketing Bestseller, <u>500 Social Media Marketing Tips.</u>

Images on Pinterest: Statistics, Case Studies, and Best Practices

Best for: infographics, photographs, graphics, and word art.

Images on Pinterest: the stats

Pinterest, the social network where users create and share pinboards from images, videos, and animated GIFs from around the web, has exploded in popularity since it launched just a few years ago. One of the reasons it is so loved by businesses as a destination for visual storytelling is its success rate in driving website traffic and converting users into making purchases. As well as visiting the site to be inspired by its wealth of visual material, millions of people use it as a place to browse and shop online.

According to SimilarWeb, an Israeli analytics firm, 58 percent of social traffic to Martha Stewart's website came from Pinterest in the six months up to November 2013, compared to 23 percent from Facebook. The Pinterest traffic amounted to 6.5% of the 5 million visits Martha receives every month. Martha Stewart's Pinterest profile is home to a wide variety of boards ranging from the promotional ("Living the Good Long Life" and "Martha's American Food" - two of her books), to helpful ("Dinner Recipes" and "My Craft Tools & Tips"), to lifestyle and inspirational pins that provide a more personal glimpse into life of a domestic goddess ("My Travels," "My Homes"). [20]

Images on Pinterest: case studies

The beauty products retailer Sephora - which uses Pinterest to showcase its products, provide make-up tutorials, and inspirational looks - revealed in May 2013 that Pinterest users spent 15 times more on Sephora products than Facebook fans. *"The reality is that when you're in the Pinterest mindset, you're actually interested in acquiring items, which is not what people go to Facebook for,"* Sephora's head of digital Julie Bornstein told VentureBeat. *"Facebook continues to be just a great customer interaction tool that gives us the real-time ability to dialog with our customer; it's a big customer-service venue for us."* [21]

While the majority (around 80%) of Pinterest's users are women, savvy marketers in all sectors have adapted to the site and used it - through original, interesting, and innovative content and themes - to appeal to an audience who might not generally be seen amongst its core demographic.

Images on Pinterest: a case study

Fetcham Park in Surrey, England, is a Grade II listed house built in 1705. After centuries as a private home, it is now family-owned by the Wilky Group, and is used as an impressive venue for hosting weddings and other events. Its director, Laura Caudery, and her team, have used Pinterest as an integral part of their visual strategy on social media (http://www.pinterest.com/fetchampark/)

"I launched Fetcham Park during a recession and had a tiny budget to work with so social media was the obvious, and only, option," says Laura. *"Fortunately, I love telling stories so I took to Twitter, Facebook, Pinterest, and Instagram to explain why I was launching a new type of wedding venue."*

Laura's approach has reaped massive rewards for the business as a whole. Fetcham Park is continually seen on the lists of 'Top Wedding Venues' in the industry's key magazines, high profile events and photo shoots have all taken place at the house, the film 'Diana' used Fetcham Park as a double for The Ritz and Laura herself has won a 'Special Recognition' award for her contribution to the wedding industry in the UK.

Boards like "Fetcham Park Weddings", "Pretty Maids All in A Row" and "Brides" all contain beautiful photos that act as subtle promotion for the venue, cleverly placing the customer at center stage (as a method of powerful social proof), whilst also giving props to some of the professional wedding photographers whose websites are often the source of the images used. Other boards like "Laura Loves" and "Inspirational Interiors" provide Pinterest users (and potential customers) with a deeper insight into the mindset of the brand, creating a sense of closeness and camaraderie.

Images on Pinterest: Best Practices

- Taller images work better than wider ones, as they have more visual impact in Pinterest's layout.
- The maximum width of images on Pinterest is 735 pixels (any wider and they will be resized when pinned or uploaded). There is no vertical length limit imposed on images.

- Add a "Pin It" button to your blog posts and images; make sure each blog post and website page has at least one great pinnable image.

- Pre-populate the description of images pinned from your website to your advantage: include the copy and hashtags in the Alt Image section.

For a much more wealthy and detailed outline of Pinterest strategy for business, read the Pinterest Tips chapter of my #1 Amazon Web Marketing Bestseller, 500 Social Media Marketing Tips.

Images on Google+: Statistics, Case Studies, and Best Practices

Best for: infographics, product shots, lifestyle and brand culture, inspirational and motivational quotes

Images on Google+: the stats

It's probably fair to say that the rise of Google+ hasn't been quite as smooth as the search giant would have wanted it to be. Lambasted as a Facebook copycat and overlooked by many, the social network still has hundreds of millions of active users, and its strong ties to search (and the SEO benefits that that brings) still make it a useful destination for business. Even if you only feed Facebook content to Google+ via third party software, it is still worth keeping an active profile there. On the visual side of the coin, statistics from October 2013 revealed that over 1.5 billion images were being uploaded to Google+ every week.[22]

Images on Google+: case study

In March 2014, the Saatchi Gallery (in conjunction with Google+) launched the Motion Photography Prize - the world's first global open entry contest to celebrate animated GIFs, especially those created using the social network's Auto Awesome feature (more details on this below). This particular type of contest was launched because it took advantage of, and showcased, an art form that has previously been pretty inaccessible. However, the rise of simple "make a GIF" tools opens the door up to almost anybody willing to give it a go. The winner and five other finalists had their work displayed in the gamous Saatchi Gallery in London. In the couple of months that it ran for, the competition attracted over 4,000 entries from 52 countries.[23] Check out the winning entry and finalists here: http://www.saatchigallery.com/mpp/

Images on Google+: best practices

- Google+ photo albums got a big overhaul last year, and thanks to the power of the company's algorithms, they're arguably the best online photo album tool out there - a place to store all of your images, which are automatically organized and edited.

- Google+'s Auto Awesome photo feature is pretty nifty. When you add new photos, Auto-enhance makes subtle adjustments (like removing red-eye and improving lighting) to help them look great. If you're not happy with the automatic changes, simply click on a photo and you'll have access to a variety of manual tools to touch up your image as you wish. In another cool feature, Auto Awesome automatically detects photos taken in quick succession, and knits them together to create an animated GIF.

- Click the Highlights tab on your Google+ photo albums to filter out duplicates, blurred images or poorly exposed photos, making it easier to find the photos that are most meaningful to you. You can then share just these very best photos with your fans.

For a much more wealthy and detailed outline of Google+ strategy for business, read the Google+ Tips chapter of my #1 Amazon Web Marketing Bestseller, <u>500 Social Media Marketing Tips.</u>

Images on Snapchat: Statistics, Case Studies, and Best Practices

Best for: photos, user-generated content, behind the scenes sneak peeks, product promotion, and more.

Images on Snapchat: the stats

Since launching in September 2011, Snapchat - the mobile app where images sent between users are "destroyed" after no longer than a 10-second viewing window (or up to 24 hours if added to a Snapchat Story) - has exploded, especially amongst teens and young adults. Before sending, images can be annotated with text, adorned with a filter, and doodled on with a rainbow of color. As of April 2014, there were 70 million monthly active Snapchat users[24], and in May 2014, these users were sending 700 million photos and videos per day, and viewing Stories some 500 million times in the same time period.[25]

While Snapchat's demographic won't suit every brand the app's throwaway content, fun culture, *and* the fact that no one knows what a snap contains before it is opened or how long it will last (meaning you'll have the user's undivided attention as they prepare to view) has made it a fresh and lucrative avenue for companies that have embraced it, including Taco Bell, GrubHub, and Lucozade. People have swarmed to Snapchat because it offers an escape from the flood of content that other social networks provide; a destination where one-to-one fun and frivolity takes center stage.

Images on Snapchat: case study

For the Super Bowl 2014, the car manufacturer Audi set out to drive awareness of its presence at the event amongst Millennials. Seeing that the app's popularity was exploding amongst teens and twenty-somethings, and it wanted to connect authentically to its audience, Audi turned to Snapchat.

In the weeks prior to the Super Bowl, fans of Audi on social networks other than Snapchat were encouraged to start following the company on the app, and - when the night of the Super Bowl arrived - they were sent snaps *"pairing stock photos with clever captions that poked fun at the banality of the typical Sunday and joked about real-time aspects of the game and the halftime show." So simple, but very effective.*[26]

http://bit.ly/audisuperbowl1
http://bit.ly/audisuperbowl2
http://bit.ly/audisuperbowl3

Independent reports suggested that Audi drove the most mentions of an online automobile maker during the Super Bowl - one third of which came off the back of its Snapchat campaign. Utilizing just a single mobile device to accept new followers, Audi managed to add more than 5,500 new followers on the Sunday evening of the Super Bowl alone (in addition to the 5,000 in the two days before), and receive more than 100,000 total views on Snapchat and 2,400 mentions on Twitter (many fans re-shared Audi's Snapchat content to their own feeds on other social networks).

Images on Snapchat: best practices

- Snapchat's largely destructible content means that your audience won't be able to return to it like they would a YouTube video or blog post, so embrace this with quick updates that capture one-off moments.

- Snapchat images are predominantly captured in portrait mode (and users will expect this when opening a snap), so consider this when creating content. If a user has to twist their phone to comprehend your photo, they'll potentially lose a significant portion of the scant time they have to view it in the first place.

- Don't be *hugely* fussy with the quality and composition of your images or the artistic merit of your doodles. Keep them eye-catching, simple, and fun.

- Want to upload a photo from your Camera Roll to use on Snapchat? There's no official way yet, but third party apps like LaterPic (iOS) will perform this function. As it is not an official app, please use it at your own risk.

Legal Considerations for Using Images on Social Media

Like much of media content hosted online, images are subject to copyright law. Although the spread and manipulation of images is almost impossible to police, there's always a slim chance that you *could* get in trouble (and from a moral standpoint, stealing is just wrong), so here are a few pointers for the use images on brand social media pages:

- Ideally, stick to making images featuring your own copyrighted materials.

- If you want to use an image that you did not create, get written releases from the people featured in it and the copyright holder. If this is not possible, link to the GIF or retweet someone else's post rather than embedding it on your own social channels. Always read the owner's terms and conditions carefully.

- The larger your business, the more likely you are to be a target of legal action if your use of images breaks copyright laws, so don't assume you can get away with posting them without permission, even if another brand already has.